ROETHLISBERGER

Pittsburgh's Own BIG BEN

SPORTS
PUBLISHING
L.L.C.

www.SportsPublishingLLC.com

ISBN: 1-59670-075-0

Printed in the United States of America

Sports Publishing L.L.C.
804 North Neil Street
Champaign, IL 61820
Phone: 1-877-424-2665 • Fax: 217-363-2073 • Web site: www.SportsPublishingLLC.com

PETER L. BANNON and JOSEPH J. BANNON SR. *publishers*

SUSAN M. MOYER *senior managing editor*

ERIN LINDEN-LEVY *photo editor*

K. JEFFREY HIGGERSON *art director*

KENNETH J. O'BRIEN and JIM HENEHAN *book design*

JOSEPH T. BRUMLEVE *cover design*

JIM HENEHAN *book layout*

KENNETH J. O'BRIEN *imaging*

KEVIN KING *vice president of sales and marketing*

NICK O'BRADOVICH *regional,*
RANDY FOUTS *national,*
MAUREY WILLIAMSON *print media and promotions managers*

Front and back cover photos by: *Jason Cohn/Icon SMI*

Contents

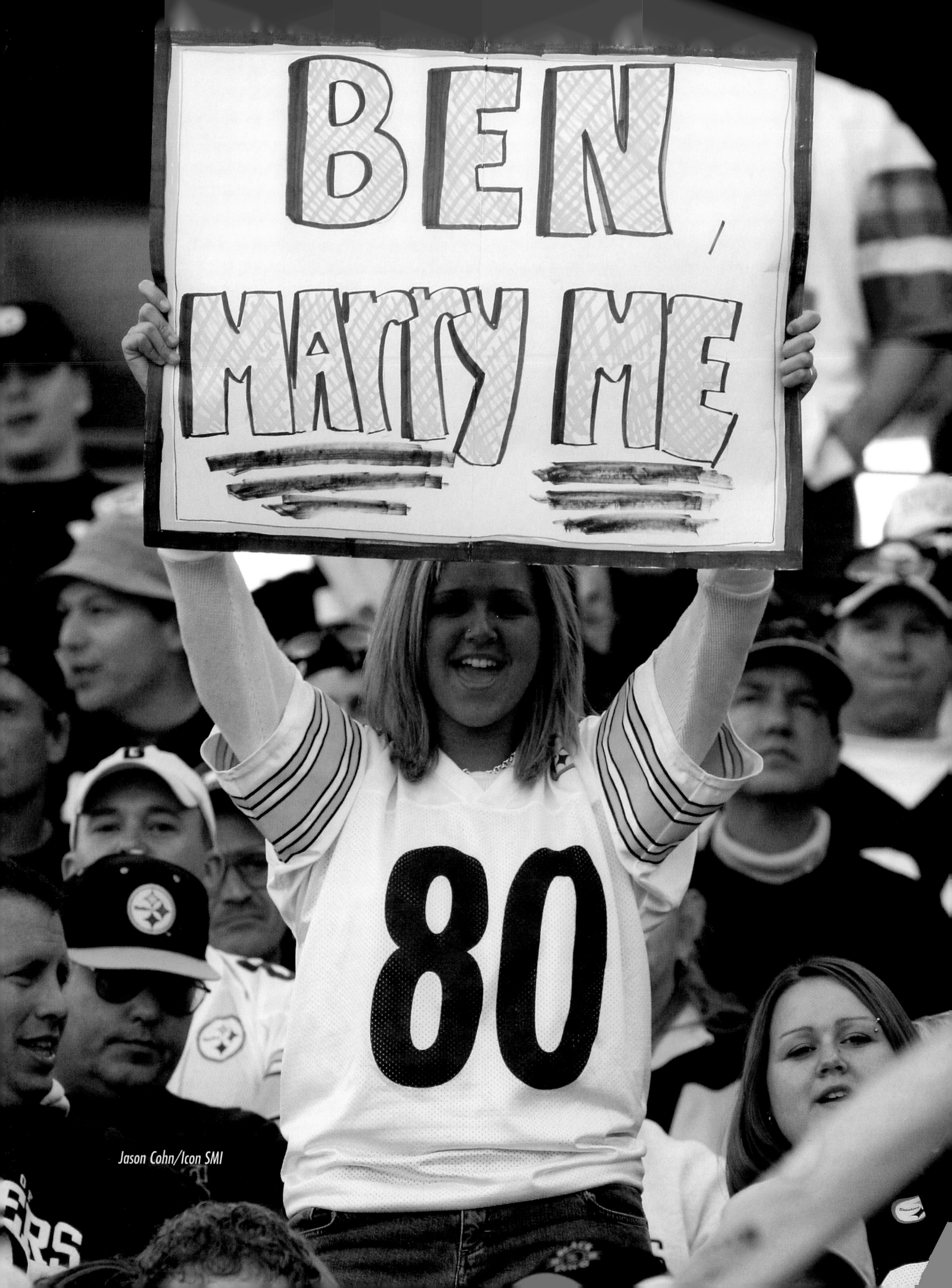

Jason Cohn/Icon SMI

December 1, 2004
Quick Update

Hey everyone,

I'm sorry it's been so long since my last entry. As I'm sure you can all imagine, I've been really busy lately. Plus, I'm having trouble getting Internet access in my new home, so that's made it even harder to keep in touch.

Joe Robbins/Getty Images

However, you are all very important to me, so I wanted to make sure I took a few minutes to touch base. I promise to write more often as soon as my schedule permits.

The support you have given me is awesome and also humbling. I'm very blessed. Steelers fans are the best fans in the world. Thanks so much from the bottom of my heart. And big thanks for continuing to support my official Website, BigBen7.com.

Well, better get back to studying for this Sunday's game. Again, God bless to every-one and thanks again for all your support. It means the world to me.

Also, I hope everyone had a great Thanksgiving. Merry Christmas and Happy Holidays to everyone if I don't get a chance to write again this month.

—Ben

Source: "Ben's Blog" on the official Ben Roethlisberger website: www.BigBen7.com

Miami Captures Its First MAC Title

RedHawks have won 12 straight

By John Seewer *Associated Press*

December 5, 2003

Ben Roethlisberger showed why so many NFL scouts are watching his every move and waiting to find out if he'll stay in college for his senior year.

Roethlisberger threw touchdown passes to four receivers Thursday night, leading No. 14 Miami University to a 49-27 win against 20th-ranked Bowling Green in the Mid-American Conference championship.

He picked apart the Falcons, spreading the ball around to nine receivers, and along the way setting a title game record with 440 passing yards.

"All I had to do was put it out there and they made the play," said Roethlisberger, who gave credit to everyone but himself.

He praised his offensive line for not allowing a sack.

"I still have a white jersey," Roethlisberger said with a grin.

He became just the second MAC quarterback to go pass for more than 4,000 yards in a season, joining Byron Leftwich.

Roethlisberger, a junior, led Miami (12-1, 9-0 MAC) to scores on its first four possessions of the second half. He sealed the victory with a 55-yard scoring pass to Calvin Murray, who found a seam along the sideline.

That put the RedHawks up 42-20 with 17 seconds left in the third quarter in only the third meeting between two MAC teams ranked in the top 25.

Roethlisberger, a semifinalist for the Davey O'Brien Award, given to the nation's top quarterback, has remained quiet all year about whether he will return to Miami University next season.

He's projected to be a top pick in the NFL draft if he comes out.

"People that know football marvel," Miami head coach Terry Hoeppner said. "It's

ABOVE: Ben Roethlisberger honed his quarterbacking skills during close games, such as this 42-37 win at

LEFT: Roethlisberger targets a receiver during a loss to Iowa. He finished his final season at Miami with 4,110 passing yards. *August Miller/Sporting News/Icon SMI*

only people who see him for the first who are surprised."

It's the first MAC title since 1986 for the RedHawks, who haven't lost since the season opener at Iowa. The last team to win all of its MAC games was Marshall in 1999.

Miami will play Louisville in the GMAC Bowl on Dec. 18.

The Falcons trailed, 21-17, at the half, despite being outgained 306 yards to 172.

But P.J. Pope fumbled on the first two possessions of the second half, giving the RedHawks the ball inside Falcons' territory each time.

And Miami took advantage.

Murray scored on a one-yard plunge and Mike Smith ran 13 yards for the first of his two touchdowns, giving the Redhawks a 35-17 lead with 4:57 left in the third quarter.

Roethlisberger, the conference's player of the year, threw four touchdown passes for the third consecutive game and completed 26 of 35 passes.

Roethlisberger now has 4,110 passing yards this year. Leftwich surpassed 4,000 twice with Marshall — in 2001 and 2002.

Roethlisberger also broke Leftwich's MAC title game record of 421 yards set in 2001.

BELOW: Evading Tar Heel defenders, Roethlisberger picks up a few yards. His agility is one of his many assets. *Icon Sports Media*

Miami's defense took away Bowling Green's short passing game and harassed quarterback Josh Harris throughout the game.

Harris, a running and passing threat, finished with 260 passing yards. He was far from sharp much of the game, completing 30 of 49 passes.

Bowling Green had no answer for Roethlisberger, who was on target all night with short throws and then went deep when the Falcons played tighter coverage.

"I can't wait to play them when he's gone," Bowling Green head coach Gregg Brandon said. "We had no answer for him. When we did pressure him, he eluded it and found receivers, and they ran past us all day."

Miami didn't take the lead until late in the second quarter.

Roethlisberger sidestepped a blitzing defender and then rolled to his left before finding Mike Larkin in the back of the end zone for a 16-yard touchdown strike that put the Redhawks ahead, 21-14, with 4:36 left in the first half. It was Roethlisberger's third touchdown pass of the half.

Bowling Green twice jumped ahead by a touchdown earlier in the half.

T.J. Carswell blocked Mike Wafzig's punt, and the Falcons recovered at the Miami 33-yard line, setting up their first score.

After moving to the 6-yard line, Harris took the snap and ran untouched into the end zone to put Bowling Green up 7-0 with 11:46 left in the first quarter.

Miami answered five plays later, when Roethlisberger found Ryne Robinson with a 53-yard touchdown pass.

Both Miami and Bowling Green were playing in the championship game for the first time.

"I can't wait to play them when he's gone. We had no answer for him."

—Bowling Green head coach Gregg Brandon

RIGHT: Ben Roethlisberger has always let his faith be his guide, on and off the field. *Icon Sports Media*

Scouting Report on Big Ben

Analysis | Agility | High School | Personal

OVERVIEW

Three-year starter who is regarded among the elite of college football ... Blessed with the size of a linebacker and the mobility of a tailback, this excellent field leader has drawn comparisons to former Buffalo Bills great Jim Kelly for his ability to remain cool under pressure and strike from anywhere on the field ... In 38 games, he rewrote virtually every school game, season and career passing records ... Completed 854 of 1,304 passes (65.5 percent) for 10,829 yards, 84 touchdowns and 34 interceptions, topping the previous all-time records of 903 pass attempts, 6,524 yards and 49 scores by Mike Bath (1997-2000), 484 pass completions by Sam Ricketts (1994-97), 27 interceptions by Larry Fortner (1975-78) and 61.6 pass-completion percentage by Terry Morris (1985-86) ... Added 246 yards and seven scores on 269 carries (0.9 avg.) ... Set another RedHawks career record with 11,075 yards in total offense, surpassing the old mark of 7,010 yards by Bath ... Became only the third player in Mid-

American Conference history to throw for over 3,000 yards in three seasons and was the 10th passer in conference annals to throw for over 10,000 yards in a career ... Became only the eighth player in school history to earn All-America honors ... Can also handle punting chores, kicking 24 times for 963 yards (40.1 avg.), with 17 attempts downed inside the 20-yard line.

ANALYSIS

Positives: Tall, mobile passer with long arms, thick legs and good quickness, balance and change-of-direction agility ... Shows good fluidity and quickness in his pass set ... Very good at reading defenses, showing patience

Dilip Vishwanat/Sporting News/Icon SMI

and the ability to pick apart zones … Has an above-average, snappy release and excellent arm strength … Generates good velocity behind his deep tosses and is equally accurate throwing from the pocket or on the move … Shows great poise in the pocket and is never rattled by pressure … While he does not have blazing speed to escape, he does show good mobility to roll away from the rush and step up to avoid the sack … Has the powerful leg drive needed to break tackles and move the chains when running with the ball … Has a compact throwing motion and excellent touch (knows when to take something off the ball, when needed) … Has a fluid over-the-top throwing motion and shows consistency throwing from the opposite hash … Will sit in and take a hit vs. the blitz, yet still make the proper throw … Would look to run at the first sign of pressure earlier in his career, but over the years, has settled down, showing patience in the pocket while trying to locate his secondary targets … Effective emergency punter who does a nice job of angling his kicks toward the sidelines.

ABOVE: Against his MAC oppenents, Roethlisberger showcased his abilities and helped solidify his value as a quarterback. *Thomas E. Witte/Icon SMI*

AGILITY TESTS

4.75 in the 40-yard dash … 340-pound bench press … 316-pound power clean … 32-inch vertical jump … 32¾-inch arm length … 9 7/8-inch hands.

HIGH SCHOOL

Attended Findlay (Ohio) High, but only played football as a senior … Still, he earned Ohio's Division I Offensive Player of the Year in 1999 … Runner-up for 1999 Mr. Football honors in Ohio … Set state records by throwing for 4,041 yards and 54 touchdowns during his senior campaign and also ran for seven scores … Named league, district and Toledo Blade Player of the Year … Helped the team compile a 23-9 record, which included two league championships and a state playoff appearance, with him as a team member … Findlay went 10-2 in 1999, advancing to second round of state playoffs before losing to Grove City … Participant in Ohio North-South and Ohio-Pennsylvania Big 33 All-Star games … Tossed two touchdowns, including the game-winner, in the North-South game … Coached by Cliff Hite … All-league and all-district performer in baseball and basketball … Team captain in all three sports … Averaged 26.5 points, nine rebounds and five assists per game as a senior point guard in basketball … A .300 hitter as a shortstop for Findlay's baseball squad … Earned second-team all-league and all-district honors in basketball and baseball.

PERSONAL

Physical Education major … Son of Ken and Brenda Roethlisberger … Born March 2, 1982 … Resides in Findlay, Ohio.

Source: NFLDraftScout.com

"[Roethlisberger] has a fluid over-the-top throwing motion and shows consistency throwing from the opposite hash … Will sit in and take a hit vs. the blitz."

Prepping for the Pros

Preparing for NFL draft is a full-time job

By Joe Kay *Associated Press*

February 28, 2004

Ben Roethlisberger's evening trips to Taco Bell and McDonald's are a thing of the past, just like his classes and textbooks.

Since he left Miami of Ohio to enter the NFL draft, the prominent quarterback has changed his life. He moved to the West Coast, overhauled his diet and started a crash course in his new career. The draft is less than two months away, and there's so much left to do — refine his body, tighten his throwing motion, take lessons in quarterback protocol.

"I'd say it's more like getting ready for a season," said Roethlisberger, who led Miami to a No. 10 final ranking with his strong arm and accuracy. "I had an idea it would be tough, but I didn't know how tough. I didn't know how much time I had to put into it."

Prepping for the pros is a full-time job nowadays, a reflection of how times have changed.

In its formative years, the NFL took a more carefree approach to sizing up picks. The process was about as intricate as thumbing through a magazine.

That's exactly what the Pittsburgh Steelers did in 1956, when they made Colorado A&M defensive back Gary Glick the first overall pick. They saw his name in a magazine's list of top players and figured: Why not?

It wasn't a big deal. Players didn't make much money—Hall of Famer Bob Lilly got a $4,000 signing bonus in 1961, for instance—and plucking them out of the draft was more akin to choosing sides on a playground.

College athletes completed their final season, played their bowl games and waited to see where they'd get picked. Eventually, teams decided to get a better idea of what they were getting by sizing them up in advance.

Still, it was fairly simple.

"Initially when we started this, guys just kind of sauntered in," said Gil Brandt, an NFL

ABOVE: Ben Roethlisberger drops back to pass while training at the EA Sports Elite 11 Quarterback Camp in San Juan Capistrano, California. *Tom Hauck/Icon SMI*

draft consultant and former Dallas Cowboys personnel director.

It gradually got more complex and took a pronounced turn in the 1990s, when player contracts soared and draft picks realized that bulging muscles could produce a bulging bank account.

Brandt was surprised when lineman Mike Mamula jumped up to the seventh overall pick in 1995 after impressing the Eagles and everyone else with his predraft workouts.

"He was probably the first guy that had done extensive training and came in and just knocked everybody's eyes out," Brandt said.

BELOW: Ben Roethlisberger shares the love at a pre-draft training camp. *Tom Hauck/Icon SMI*

"The stakes for a player like Ben are much higher and the dynamic is different than it would be for a typical player."

—Agent Leigh Steinberg

"He was thought to be maybe a third- or fourth-round pick before that."

Now everybody has to keep up. Agents line up clients with trainers and coaches. Players go through preparatory camps, learning how to look good at workouts and come across well in interviews. Nothing is overlooked.

"It's like parents getting their kids tutored to take the ACT or the SAT," Brandt said.

There's a lot more at stake than a scholarship. Last year, first-round draft picks got $210 million in signing bonuses. Moving just a few spots in the draft can mean millions of dollars.

Even a top prospect like Roethlisberger has a lot at stake. He and Eli Manning are expected to be the top quarterbacks taken in the draft on April 24. Quarterbacks get the big bucks and the biggest expectations.

"The stakes for a player like Ben are much higher and the dynamic is different than it would be for a typical player," said agent Leigh Steinberg, who has represented eight No. 1 overall picks.

Heisman Trophy winner Carson Palmer got $14 million in bonuses last year when the

RIGHT: Big Ben sizes up the competition at the EA Sports Elite 11 Quarterback Camp. *Tom Hauck/Icon SMI*

Bengals made him the top overall pick. San Diego gets to choose first this time around.

Picking franchise quarterbacks is a risky business. Most first-rounders don't develop into Pro Bowl passers. If a team guesses right, it has a chance to be successful for years. If it guesses wrong—or puts the pick in the wrong setting—the team will pay for years.

Roethlisberger spent the last two months getting ready to make a good impression on teams looking for a franchise player. Roethlisberger, who was one of Ohio's top prep passers at Findlay High School, moved to Newport Beach, California, so he could work out every day in warmer weather.

His daily routine includes an hour of weight training, an hour or more working out with a quarterback coach, then a session at Steinberg's office getting mail and doing interviews. There's another hour-long workout to improve his speed before the day is done.

"There's very little sitting down," said Roethlisberger, who left Miami after his junior season. "Very rarely do I not have any workouts. Sunday is my one day off."

There's also some travel. Steinberg took him to the Senior Bowl to meet NFL scouts, coaches and general managers. He also brought Roethlisberger to Super Bowl week in Houston, helping him get another foot in the door while getting a look at the mass media.

"I was kind of star-struck to see people like Ronnie Lott, Joe Montana, Howie Long, Cris Carter, Warren Moon," Roethlisberger said. "I had posters of these guys."

Roethlisberger worked out at the scouting combine in Indianapolis this month. There will be more workouts in the coming weeks, as teams with top picks narrow their choices.

In the meantime, Roethlisberger's daily schedule is crammed.

"Everything is a little overwhelming, but it's starting to sink in that this is kind of my life now and it's going to be my life," he said.

> **"There's very little sitting down. Very rarely do I not have any workouts. Sunday is my one day off."**
>
> —Ben Roethlisberger

Tom Hauck/Icon SMI

Proving Himself

"Roethlisberger: Manning, Rivers have nothing on me."

By Alan Robinson *Associated Press*

April 26, 2004

Ben Roethlisberger arrived Monday in Pittsburgh as the No. 3 quarterback in the NFL draft and, for now, no better than No. 3 on the Steelers' depth chart.

He doesn't expect either situation to last very long. Roethlisberger, only the second quarterback drafted in the first round by Pittsburgh in 33 years, didn't predict he would beat out incumbent Tommy Maddox or back-up Charlie Batch immediately. He didn't promise to have better rookie-year statistics than Mississippi's Eli Manning or North Carolina State's Philip Rivers, the two quarterbacks drafted ahead of him.

But he said he lacks nothing Manning and Rivers possess — he dismisses talk the Manning family lineage gives Eli an edge — and is eager to show it. Even if he must wait a little longer to play than Manning does with the Giants or Rivers does with the Chargers.

"Eli's been getting a lot of hype leading up to this, but I said coming in it all boils down to this: it's just football," Roethlisberger said. "That's what I've been wanting to do for a long time, just get on the field and start playing."

Roethlisberger didn't criticize Rivers or Manning, but said, "I think I bring a little more athleticism than both of them, but I guess we'll have to wait and see.

"Everyone seems to think they have better systems, better teams they played on in college, were born into a football family," said Roethlisberger, who played at Miami of Ohio. "Once I get the field, my will to win is much greater than both of them."

Roethlisberger has already created more buzz in Pittsburgh than any Steelers quarterback draft pick since Terry Bradshaw in 1970. The Steelers haven't yet started selling

ABOVE: Although Eli Manning was drafted ahead of him, Roethlisberger believes his heart and athleticism will elevate him on the field. *Bob Leverone/Sporting News/Icon SMI*

too-small uniform for Monday's photo shoot.

Now, they've got to find out how Roethlisberger fits into an already crowded quarterback mix.

Maddox, a starter who is earning backup-like wages, apparently wanted to meet Monday with Steelers chairman Dan Rooney and coach Bill Cowher to discuss his future, however short it may be.

But there was no meeting, with Rooney saying one was never planned, and no hint when there might be one. It's possible Maddox and Cowher might talk on the phone later this week, though Cowher prefers to talk in person.

While Maddox is underpaid for an NFL starter at $750,000, he now has little bargaining power. The Steelers won't pay Roethlisberger millions to sit very long, and that means Maddox may remain the starter only one more season — or less. Maddox could find himself playing this season for the chance to earn a contract elsewhere next year.

Roethlisberger was diplomatic when discussing playing time, at least for this season.

"I'm willing to do whatever the team asks of me, whether that's play right away or sit,"

Roethlisberger's No. 7 jersey, but no doubt they will quickly order up a batch to satisfy fan demand.

They might want to order a few in extra-extra large, too; obviously not accustomed to having 6-foot-5, 240-pound quarterbacks, the Steelers badly underestimated Roethlisberger's size and gave him a much-he said. "I want to talk to Tommy and Charlie a little bit about what's going on. Whatever they're willing to help me with, I'm going to take it all in."

Wide receiver Plaxico Burress, who is signed only through this season and could also be playing for a contract, is curious to see how the quarterback situation plays out. Cowher hasn't ruled out Roethlisberger's starting this season.

"The best man's going to win. That's the reason why we have minicamps and training camps," Burress said. "I don't really have an idea who it's going to be, but when you bring a quarterback in that high, I guess it kind of sends a red light up to Tommy. I guess he's kind of down about the situation, but I've been playing with him for two years and I'm sure he'll step up and defend his position."

BELOW: From left: Robert Gallery, DeAngelo Hall, Eli Manning, Ben Roethlisberger, Roy Williams and Kellen Winslow II pose during the 2004 NFL Draft at Madison Square Garden. *Bob Leverone/Sporting News/Icon SMI*

Big Ben Signs Contract

Steelers give Roethlisberger largest bonus in team history

By Alan Robinson *Associated Press*

August 4, 2004

With one stroke of a pen, Ben Roethlisberger made more money than the greatest Pittsburgh Steelers ever made.

Roethlisberger's agent, Leigh Steinberg, may be as biased as anyone, but he says the Steelers will someday consider the $9,000,900 in bonuses they'll pay the rookie quarterback a tremendous bargain. Even if it is far more money than Hall of Famers Terry Bradshaw, Joe Greene, Jack Ham and Jack Lambert — the icons of the Steelers' franchise — made during their entire careers.

"This is a franchise quarterback," Steinberg said Tuesday. "I think he's a Troy Aikman, John Elway type of quarterback. He's that good."

He's also that rich. Even before playing his first down with the Steelers, Roethlisberger was given the largest bonus in team history. Previously, the largest bonus was the $8.1 million paid former starting quarterback Kordell Stewart, another Steinberg client, in 1999.

Roethlisberger's six-year contract consists of $22,269,500 of salaries and various bonuses and $17,730,500 in incentives, including

"Now that the contract's out of the way, it's time for football. I'm ready to do whatever is asked of me."

—Ben Roethlisberger

ABOVE: Commissioner Paul Tagliabue presents Ben Roethlisberger with his Steelers jersey after Pittsburgh

$4,875,000 in playing time bonuses easily reachable for a starting quarterback.

Because he's expected to be a backup this season, Roethlisberger could collect bonuses of $600,000 (signing bonus, payable immediately), $1,172,000 (roster bonus, payable by Aug. 10) and $7,237,000 (option bonus, payable March 5) even before he has started a game.

The Steelers initially wanted to give Roethlisberger a smaller bonus than Houston cornerback Dunta Robinson got but more than the $7.25 million that No. 12 pick Jonathan Vilma got from the New York Jets.

Roethlisberger is the first quarterback drafted by the Steelers in the first round since Mark Malone in 1980. He is expected to back up Tommy Maddox this season, but could move into the starting job as early as 2005.

Earlier this year, Maddox signed an incentives-driven contract extension through 2007 that included a $2 million pay hike this season.

Delane B. Rouse/Icon SMI

Maddox will go back to making backup-type money if Roethlisberger becomes the starter.

"Now that the contract's out of the way, it's time for football," Roethlisberger said. "I'm ready to do whatever is asked of me, whether it's be the backup or play third string."

To get a larger bonus, Roethlisberger agreed to play this season for the minimum salary of $230,000.

"We felt that quarterbacks deserve a premium, and the Steelers ultimately agreed," said Steinberg, who flew to Pittsburgh on Sunday night to accelerate the talks with Steelers negotiator Omar Khan and team president Art Rooney II. "A potential franchise quarterback always is a special sort of player to deal with."

For now, Roethlisberger is just another player. Barely three hours after arriving in camp, he attended a quarterbacks meeting. He was scheduled to take part in two practices

BELOW: New Steeler Ben Roethlisberger smiles as he is interviewed on the radio. *Bob Leverone/Sporting News/Icon SMI*

Wednesday, one before a crowd that could reach 10,000 at a local high school stadium.

Some of his game crowds at Miami (Ohio) weren't much bigger than that.

"I'm excited, nervous, all the same feelings I had at minicamp," he said. "Once I get out and throw the first couple of passes, it will be a relief and I'm sure it will come back to me."

Roethlisberger was the third quarterback drafted in April, behind the Giants' Eli Manning and the Chargers' Philip Rivers, but some scouts believe he has the most potential of the group—even if it takes him longer to play. The 6-foot-5, 240-pound Roethlisberger completed 854 of 1,304 passes for 10,829 yards at Miami of the Mid-American Conference, with 84 touchdown passes and 34 interceptions.

Despite a holdout longer than either he or the Steelers wanted, Roethlisberger wound up missing only four practices.

"Every meeting, every practice is invaluable, and hopefully he'll get caught up as much as possible," coach Bill Cowher said. "Obviously, he'll need to spend some extra time getting caught up on the things we've put in, because there are new things every night."

Roethlisberger's base salaries will be $230,000 (2004), $305,000 (2005), $655,000 (2006), $1,026,000 (2007), $1,356,000 (2008) and $1,707,000 (2009), which is payable on March 5, 2009.

His bonuses include $250,000 for rookie of the year, $500,000 for the Pro Bowl and $4,750,000 for finishing in the top five in various QB statistical categories. His playing time bonuses increase with time played and could reach as much as $975,000 a year if the Steelers make the playoffs.

Training Camp Debut

Roethlisberger shows no hesitancy during first Steelers practice

By Alan Robinson *Associated Press*

August 4, 2004

No matter how many passes he completed in college, no matter how many millions he now has in the bank, Ben Roethlisberger was just like any other football player on his first official day in a new uniform.

Nervous. Really, really nervous. "Without question," Roethlisberger said Wednesday after his first training camp practice with the Pittsburgh Steelers. "It felt like the first day of minicamp all over again. Tommy [Maddox] and I were laughing about it. You need to get out there and get the first play out [of the way]."

That first play was nothing remarkable for the most-watched Steelers rookie quarterback since, well, Terry Bradshaw in 1970. Lining up under center from the 20-yard line in a 7-on-7 passing drill, Roethlisberger overthrew wide receiver Plaxico Burress near the goal line.

On the next play, Roethlisberger threaded a pass through heavy coverage to Burress at the 1.

So much for nerves.

"I had a chance to throw to Plax for the first time and I overthrew him because I was so excited, so I came back and got him the next time," Roethlisberger said. "The butterflies were gone and it was good to get back out there."

The former Miami (Ohio) star missed the first four practices of camp before signing a contract that guarantees him $9 million in bonuses by March. Still, he spent more than a month with the team during minicamp and at the voluntary coaching sessions this spring, and he picked up much of the offense then.

Quarterbacks coach Mark Whipple already is holding extra meetings with the rookie to get him up to speed.

ABOVE: Rookie QB Ben Roethlisberger takes a snap during the Pittsburgh minicamp. *Jason Cohn/Icon SMI*

ABOVE: Coach Bill Cowher has high hopes for Roethlisberger and the Steelers in 2004.
Jason Cohn/Icon SMI

"I don't think I'm very far behind at all; everything has already been installed," Roethlisberger said. "I'm more behind being out here on the field, throwing with the guys. ... But I don't feel like I lost too much time. It's just getting back out there and getting into the groove of things."

The Steelers don't plan to rush Roethlisberger during his rookie year, giving him plenty of time to settle in and get comfortable as Maddox plays. Roethlisberger will get off the bench only if Maddox is injured or badly underperforms and, even if that happens, veteran quarterback Charlie Batch might play ahead of him.

But if Roethlisberger keeps displaying the in-huddle presence, the confidence and arm strength he showed on his first day of training camp, the Steelers realize it will be difficult to keep him on the bench for very long after this season.

Jason Cohn/Icon SMI

"I had a chance to throw to Plax for the first time and I overthrew him because I was so excited, so I came back and got him the next time. The butterflies were gone and it was good to get back out there."

—Ben Roethlisberger

"I thought he looked pretty good," Burress said. "He'll probably need a few days (to settle in), and he's probably trying to make perfect throws right now."

Roethlisberger's arrival created no visible tension or competition in camp—a contrast, perhaps, to the rookie Eli Manning vs. veteran Kurt Warner duel on the New York Giants. Maddox realizes that the Steelers didn't bring in Roethlisberger to keep him benched long-term, but he has been supportive of the rookie.

"I think everybody's been looking forward to this season," Maddox said. "We have a lot of talent on this team and people who want to win. I think we're going to surprise people."

For now, Roethlisberger would prefer no surprises.

"Now it's strictly football and there's nothing else to worry about," he said. "I can just concentrate on what I have to do."

Jason Cohn/Icon SMI

Jason Cohn/Icon SMI

Taking the Reins

Cowher to Steelers: "Don't worry about new QB, worry about your own play"

By Alan Robinson *Associated Press*

September 21, 2004

Coach Bill Cowher's message for any Pittsburgh Steelers player fretting that rookie Ben Roethlisberger now is the starting quarterback: Don't worry about him, worry about yourself.

The Steelers' play during their 30-13 loss Sunday in Baltimore was so deficient that the early-season move from injured starter Tommy Maddox to Roethlisberger isn't atop Cowher's long list of concerns. "I think it is not so much what we are doing with Ben, it is that everyone around him right now has to make sure that they hold up their end of the bargain," Cowher said Tuesday. "I think Ben will be fine. No one has to do anything special. Right now, everybody has to pick up their game."

Maddox won't throw for approximately six weeks because of ligament and tendon tears in his right elbow, though that is only an approximate timetable and he is soliciting a second opinion from an elbow specialist. Once

> "I think Ben will be fine. No one has to do anything special. Right now, everybody has to pick up their game."
>
> —Bill Cowher

ABOVE: Ben Roethlisberger receives some instruction from Bill Cowher during a game. Coach Cowher has confidence in the abilities of his young quarterback. *Aaron Josefczyk/Icon SMI*

ABOVE: Tommy Maddox was slated to be the Steelers' starting QB, but he watches from the sideline due to an elbow injury. *Jason Cohn/Icon SMI*

Maddox is cleared to throw, the Steelers will determine when he can play again.

On Tuesday, the Steelers brought back Mike Quinn as their No. 3 quarterback—the same role he had in 1997—by adding him to the practice squad. Brian St. Pierre, who began the season on the practice squad, now is the No. 2 quarterback.

Quinn was waived by the Denver Broncos late in training camp. He has been with the Steelers, Cowboys, Dolphins, Texans and Broncos since 1997, but has thrown only three passes during that span, completing two.

Randy Litzinger/Icon SMI

Into the Fire

Despite wind, rain, delay, Roethlisberger a winner in first NFL start

By Alan Robinson *Associated Press*

September 28, 2004

Ben Roethlisberger passed the audition. The weather—a first-half downpour that trailed the back edge of a hurricane—couldn't have been much worse. The distractions—a 7 1/2-hour delay and a loss of power in the team hotel—could have been unsettling. No matter, Roethlisberger became the first Steelers rookie to win his initial NFL start since Mike Kruczek in 1976. And unlike Kruczek, Roethlisberger wasn't backed by the defending Super Bowl champions.

Despite being intercepted on his first throw and leading an offense that scored only three points in the first half, Roethlisberger played just well enough Sunday night to lead the Steelers to a 13-3 victory at Miami.

No doubt when Roethlisberger relates the story to his relatives some day in the future, they won't believe the part about the hurricane that had just departed or the ankle-deep water on the field.

"Talk about getting thrown into the fire," said Roethlisberger, using a not-so-fitting analogy.

It was more like getting thrown into a monsoon. The field was so slick and the rain was so hard during the first half, it seemed unlikely either team would get much going on offense. But the rain let up enough for Roethlisberger to find Plaxico Burress on a 42-yard reception that set up the first of two Jeff Reed field goals, a 40-yarder, and the Steelers never trailed.

In the second half, Roethlisberger finished the only touchdown drive of the game by hitting Hines Ward for a seven-yard score just inside the right front end-zone pylon on a perfectly thrown pass.

ABOVE: Ben Roethlisberger warms up prior to the game against the Dolphins in Miami. *Gary Rothstein/Icon SMI*

LEFT: Duce Staley's late-blooming running game forced Roethlisberger to carry the team for much of the night.
Gary Rothstein/Icon SMI

Call it the one perfect play of an imperfect game, but coach Bill Cowher liked what he saw of a quarterback who figures to be the starter for at least five more weeks while Tommy Maddox heals from a right elbow injury.

"He never lost his composure and he played liked I thought he would," Cowher said. "This is a great learning experience. ... After the first play when he threw an interception, he bounced back and made good decisions and gave guys a chance to make some plays."

With the Steelers' running game not doing much until late in the game, when the rain let up and Duce Staley got most of his 22 carries for 101 yards, Roethlisberger was forced to shoulder most of the offense for three quarters.

"It was rough for a little bit, but he held his own," Ward said. "He came out and did a tremendous job. He settled down. ... He played his heart out."

Ward also said the first-round draft pick didn't take long to take control of the huddle.

"He just enjoys playing."
—Bill Cowher

BELOW: Duce Staley stays just ahead of Miami's Antuan Edwards. *Gary Rothstein/Icon SMI*

"For a rookie, I figured he was a little shy for a little bit, but we have a great group of guys in the huddle," Ward said. "If he's not saying anything to someone, someone else will take control and step up."

Roethlisberger said his teammates didn't treat him like a rookie.

"They'll come up to me with suggestions such as 'speak up' or other little things that will make a difference," he said.

The Steelers will try now to do something they couldn't do a year ago: make something of consecutive home games following a 2-1 start. A year ago, they were taken apart by Tennessee (30-13) and Cleveland (33-13) at home and went on to finish 6-10.

This time, they've got the Bengals (1-2) and Browns (1-2) the next two weeks in what would appear to be winnable games, even with a rookie quarterback leading them.

"He just enjoys playing," Cowher said.

"It was rough for a little bit, but he held his own. He came out and did a tremendous job. He settled down. ... He played his heart out."

—Hines Ward

Randy Litzinger/Icon SMI

Learning the System

In a rush: Steelers look to run it up against Bengals, take heat off rookie QB

By Alan Robinson *Associated Press*

October 1, 2004

When Ben Roethlisberger was a senior at Miami (Ohio), he made the short drive to the Cincinnati Bengals' training camp. Watching practice from a roped-off area, he remembers thinking they were doing exactly the right thing with quarterback Carson Palmer.

Rather than throwing the No. 1 draft pick into the lineup, unprepared and unequipped to deal with sophisticated NFL defenses, the Bengals gave Palmer time to learn their system and the league while Jon Kitna played. The Pittsburgh Steelers intended to bring Roethlisberger along the same proven path that NFL star quarterbacks Chad Pennington and Steve McNair once traveled ahead of Palmer. They had veteran quarterbacks Tommy Maddox and Charlie Batch ahead of him, so they felt no need to rush their first-round draft pick no matter how much his

poise, maturity and strong right arm impressed them.

So much for planning. So much for patience.

When the Bengals (1-2) and Steelers (2-1) meet Sunday, Palmer and Roethlisberger will be on the field—Palmer by design, Roethlisberger out of necessity. For a matchup that figures to take place for years in the AFC North, the only surprise is it came so soon.

Even if the man who chose to sit Palmer all last season doesn't think it's a calamity for the Steelers that injuries to Maddox and Batch conspired to make Roethlisberger their starter for at least another month.

"That was not quite their plan, (but) it is a good thing," Bengals coach Marvin Lewis said. "I don't think it will be too big for him. Every chance I've had to be around him, to lis-

ten to him, watch his mannerisms and see how he presents himself ... I think he will be fine."

Roethlisberger did something in his first career start Palmer couldn't in his third start Sunday: lead a touchdown drive. It was only one touchdown during a rainy, 13-3 victory in Miami, but it helped make for the first successful debut start by a Steelers rookie quarterback since Mike Kruczek in 1976.

Roethlisberger's numbers weren't sensational (12 of 22 for 163 yards, one touchdown and one interception) but he hardly looked overwhelmed—especially considering his first NFL start came barely 12 hours after a hurricane swept through the city in which he was playing.

He didn't lose the game, or his sense of humor.

"It's good to get that game out of the way, in case we ever play in a hurricane again—which I doubt we will," Roethlisberger said.

To protect Roethlisberger, the Steelers simplified an offense that relied mostly on the run and leaned on a defense that gave Miami virtually nothing. They will try the same formula against the Bengals, who have proven incapable of sustaining any offense or stopping the run on defense.

The Bengals have gone eight quarters and 30 possessions without a touchdown behind Palmer, who threw three interceptions and was sacked four times in a 23-9 loss to Baltimore. That lack of production is making it impossible to compensate for a defense that is allowing 166 yards rushing per game and a league-worst 5.6 yards per carry.

"I think (the Jets') Curtis Martin and (the Ravens') Jamal Lewis had a lot to do with that," Steelers coach Bill Cowher said.

LEFT: Ben Roethlisberger is exceeding expectations in his first season and is often compared to Carson Palmer of the Cincinnati Bengals, a prized rookie QB out of USC in 2003. *Jason Cohn/Icon SMI*

Randy Litzinger/Icon SMI

Still, the Steelers' Duce Staley is coming off a 101-yard game against Miami and is likely to get the ball frequently on the early downs—not just to test that defense, but to keep from forcing Roethlisberger to throw in unfavorable situations.

"We are going to try to establish the running game and establish the Pittsburgh offense," Roethlisberger said.

As if the Bengals weren't in bad enough shape defensively, they'll be without middle linebacker Nate Webster (knee) for the rest of the season. Third-round draft pick Caleb Miller takes his place.

While the season isn't a month old, it's a potentially pivotal game. The Steelers also were 2-1 a year ago, only to see their season unravel with consecutive home losses to

> **"I don't think it will be too big for him. Every chance I've had to be around him, to listen to him, watch his mannerisms and see how he presents himself ... I think he will be fine."**
>
> —Bengals coach Marvin Lewis

Tennessee and Cleveland that eventually led to their 6-10 finish.

They are at home for four of their next five games, creating the potential for a fast start.

"I think sometimes last year we looked at our schedule and we kind of felt like we were going to win ballgames," wide receiver Hines Ward said. "This year we taking the approach to just take care of this week. There are no sorry teams in the NFL."

The Bengals try to avoid being 1-3 going into their bye week. They had the same record last year, then missed the playoffs despite winning seven of nine games.

"It's a very important game," wide receiver Chad Johnson said. "It puts a lot of pressure on us as a team. We don't want to fall too far behind and have to climb out of a hole like we did last year."

Drew Hallowell/Icon SMI

Big Ben Shows Poise

Steelers 28, Bengals 17

By Alan Robinson *Associated Press*

October 3, 2004

The Pittsburgh Steelers don't need quarterback Ben Roethlisberger to win games, just to keep from losing them. With victories in two promising starts, he's doing just fine.

Roethlisberger, showing uncommon poise for a rookie who wasn't expected to play this season, twice rallied the Steelers (3-1) and Duce Staley ran for 123 yards in a 28-17 victory Sunday over the Cincinnati Bengals (1-3). "You can just see him coming into his own," wide receiver Plaxico Burress said. "He doesn't let anything bother him, and that's what I like about him."

Roethlisberger went 17 of 25 for 174 yards, a touchdown and no interceptions to better Carson Palmer in a QB duel that may be repeated for years in the AFC North. Palmer drove the Bengals to touchdowns on their opening drive of each half, but ended the game with consecutive interceptions, giving him seven in four starts.

Palmer's former Southern Cal roommate, Troy Polamalu, finished it off with a 26-yard interception return for a touchdown. Jerome Bettis had given the Steelers a 21-17 lead with

"You can just see him coming into his own. He doesn't let anything bother him, and that's what I like about him."

—Plaxico Burress

ABOVE: Coach Bill Cowher is pleased with the maturity and ability of his young QB, Ben Roethlisberger.
Jason Cohn/Icon SMI

just over nine minutes remaining with his second short-range touchdown.

Already, some Bengals fans are questioning the decision to bench Jon Kitna, who threw 26 touchdown passes last season as the NFL Comeback Player of the Year, and play Palmer.

"I'm not concerned with what people say," Palmer said. "I'm only worried about what the coaches and players think. I'm going about my business, trying to get better from week to week."

Roethlisberger, replacing the injured Tommy Maddox, is the first Steelers rookie quarterback to win his first two starts since Mike Kruczek won nine in a row in place of the injured Terry Bradshaw in 1976. The difference is that Roethlisberger isn't being supported by arguably the best defense in NFL history.

"He's 2-0 and he's only going to get better," wide receiver Hines Ward said. "He's still a rookie and he still makes mistakes. Overall, he's making more good plays than bad plays and I think he's getting more comfortable."

"I have not mastered this offense by any means," Roethlisberger said. "But the thing is

ABOVE: Ben Roethlisberger completed 17 of 25 passes against the Bengals and threw no interceptions.
Jason Cohn/Icon SMI

we got the victory. You lead the team when they need it the most, you go down the field and score."

Palmer, who was 20 of 37 for 164 yards with two interceptions, showed why the Bengals drafted him No. 1 last year and why he still has some maturing to do.

Palmer went four for four for 37 yards on third downs on a drive ended by Rudi Johnson's two-yard touchdown run, giving Cincinnati a 17-14 lead early in the third. Johnson ran for 123 yards in his fifth career 100-yard game and first of the season.

But with the Bengals in position to beat a winning-record team on the road for the first time in 42 games, a streak that dates to a December 1990 victory in Pittsburgh, they couldn't score again.

"We've got to get it together fast," wide receiver Chad Johnson said. "We're behind the 8-

ball. We're in a position we don't want to be in."

After the Bengals twice couldn't score after advancing to at least the Pittsburgh 40, the Steelers drove 89 yards for Bettis' go-ahead score. The key play was a 21-yard pass interference call on Tory James against Plaxico Burress, with TV replays appearing to show little contact by James.

"Tory was just playing the ball, and he has a right to the ball," linebacker Kevin Hardy said.

The Bengals couldn't hold a 7-0 lead after Staley's first fumble led to Jeremi Johnson's touchdown on a two-yard pass midway through the first quarter—the Cincinnati offense's first touchdown in 32 possessions over three games.

The Steelers, winning consecutive games for the first time since capturing their final three to close the 2002 regular season, quickly answered. Roethlisberger's 30-yard completion to Burress set up Bettis' two-yard touchdown run, and Roethlisberger later found Verron Haynes on an 11-yard pass play for Haynes' first career touchdown.

"He's 2-0 and he's only going to get better. He's still a rookie and he still makes mistakes. Overall, he's making more good plays than bad plays and I think he's getting more comfortable."

—Hines Ward

ABOVE: Vernon Haynes celebrates his first career touchdown—an 11-yard pass from Roethlisberger. *Jason Cohn/Icon SMI*

Roethlisberger Wins Three

Steelers 34, Browns 23

By Alan Robinson *Associated Press*

October 10, 2004

The Pittsburgh Steelers keep telling themselves Ben Roethlisberger is only a rookie and they can't expect too much. Apparently, their opponents are unwisely taking the same approach.

Roethlisberger, becoming more comfortable and more productive with each start, confused Cleveland with his running and creativity and the Steelers won their third in a row behind the rookie quarterback, beating the Browns 34-23 Sunday. Browns safety Earl Little said beforehand that Roethlisberger wasn't Cleveland's biggest worry because the Steelers are asking him only to manage their offense and keep from making mistakes. Turns out the Browns might have underestimated him just a little.

The 6-foot-5, 240-pound Roethlisberger was 16 for 21 for 231 yards, a touchdown pass and a TD run. And to think he might not be

playing if starter Tommy Maddox hadn't hurt his right elbow Sept. 19 against Baltimore.

"Every week is getting better," Roethlisberger said. "It's all just starting to come together."

Just as it is for the Steelers, who are 4-1 for only the third time in 22 seasons after going 6-10 last season. Duce Staley complemented Roethlisberger by scoring on a 25-yard run while gaining 117 yards, his third consecutive 100-yard game.

The Browns (2-3) missed a chance to move over .500 after multiple games for the first time since late in the 2002 season and dropped two games behind Pittsburgh in the AFC North.

Some NFL scouts felt Roethlisberger needed the most polishing of the three quarterbacks chosen early in the April draft. Yet while the Giants' more-publicized Eli Manning and the Chargers' Philip Rivers are sitting, Roethlisberger is only the sixth rookie quarter-

ABOVE: Roethlisberger takes the snap from center Jeff Hartings during the Steelers 34-23 win over the

ABOVE: Displaying another offensive weapon, Roethlisberger scrambles for a six-yard TD. *Aaron Josefczyk/Icon SMI*

back to win his first three starts since the NFL merger in 1970. Steelers rookie Mike Kruczek was 6-0 in 1976.

"He made a couple of plays that, yeah, you definitely look at and say, 'Boy, this guy can play,'" Steelers center Jeff Hartings said. "The way he throws on the run, being able to stop and sling it 40-50 yards, that's just natural abil-ity. I think Pittsburgh's going to be happy to have him."

With the score tied at 7, Roethlisberger scrambled to elude Ebenezer Ekuban, then was flattened by Orpheus Roye's hit, yet still found Plaxico Burress for 51 yards to the Cleveland 9. A play later, Roethlisberger, apparently not rattled by the hit, powered up the middle on a six-yard TD run — matching the number of scoring runs the less-mobile Maddox has in 33 games with Pittsburgh.

"He made some throws," Roye said. "He played like a veteran. You couldn't tell he was a rookie."

The threat Roethlisberger created by his running also led to his 37-yard scoring pass to Burress that made it 24-10 midway through the third. Roethlisberger rolled out of the pocket, momentarily freezing the defense and allowing Burress to slip five yards behind cornerback Anthony Henry for an unguarded touchdown. Burress made six catches for 136 yards.

"A lot of those plays aren't called, but the linemen are doing a great job of blocking and the wide receivers are getting open,"

BELOW: Duce Staley adds to his total yardage with this run. He finished the game with 117 yards.
Aaron Josefczyk/Icon SMI

Roethlisberger said. "For me it's easy, all I've got to do is run and throw the football."

While Roethlisberger stayed poised, Browns free agent quarterback Jeff Garcia still looked uncomfortable out of the 49ers' West Coast offense despite dodging a heavy pass rush to throw for 210 yards. Coach Butch Davis, 1-7 against the Steelers, made no move to replace him with Kelly Holcomb, who passed for 663 yards in his two career starts against Pittsburgh.

BELOW: Ben Roethlisberger keeps his cool under heavy pressure and looks for an open man. The rookie QB completed 16 of 21 passes for 231 yards against the Browns. *Aaron Josefczyk/Icon SMI*

> ## "He made some throws. He played like a veteran. You couldn't tell he was a rookie."
>
> —Orpheus Roye

After Chris Crocker's 20-yard interception return for a touchdown in the first quarter, Cleveland's only scoring consisted only of Phil Dawson's three field goals until Andre Davis' seven-yard touchdown catch in the fourth quarter. Dawson is 11 of 11 this season and has made 21 in a row since Oct. 19, 2003, to prop up an offense that hasn't scored a first-half touchdown this season.

"If you settle for field goals instead of touchdowns, you never create any heat on them," Garcia said.

ABOVE: Plaxico Burress and Roethlisberger celebrate after Big Ben found Burress for a 37-yard touchdown.
Jason Cohn/Icon SMI

Aaron Josefczyk/Icon SMI

Big Ben Another Marino?

Parcells: Roethlisberger best rookie QB he's seen in years

By Alan Robinson *Associated Press*

October 13, 2004

Asked to name the last rookie quarterback who impressed him as much as the Steelers' Ben Roethlisberger, Dallas Cowboys coach Bill Parcells immediately dropped a name familiar to most Pittsburghers.

Dan Marino. "He is the best (quarterback) prospect I have seen in 10 or 15 years," Parcells said Wednesday during a conference call. "I have not seen anybody come in the league like that. The only guy that I can say came in, and the first year started playing like he is playing, is Dan Marino."

The Steelers, then on the downslide following their Super Bowl successes of the 1970s, regretted for years not drafting Marino, a local college star, in 1983. Partly because of that decision, they never did find a comparable replacement for Hall of Fame quarterback Terry Bradshaw, winning only two playoff games from 1980 through 1993.

Parcells doesn't think the Steelers will ever regret taking Roethlisberger, who is 3-0 as a starter since replacing the injured Tommy Maddox. The Steelers (4-1) play at Dallas (2-2) on Sunday.

Roethlisberger enjoyed one of the best all-around games in years by a Steelers quarterback Sunday, throwing for a touchdown, running for another while constantly keeping Cleveland's defense off-balance with his scrambling in a 34-23 victory.

"He is out of the pocket throwing 50-yard passes right on the money," Parcells said. "It is not going to be without growing pains, but I think he is in an ideal situation. They have good balance on offense. They are running the ball well. They have a good receiving corps. ...

Aaron Josefczyk/Icon SMI

"I am telling you, I am very, impressed, and it is not just because he is an opponent."

—Dallas Cowboys coach Bill Parcells

I am telling you, I am very, very impressed, and it is not just because he is an opponent."

Roethlisberger respectfully accepted the praise but detected a veteran coach employing some pregame psychological trickery.

"He's been around for a long time. He knows what he's doing. He has no problem putting those [comments] out there and trying to get inside someone's head," Roethlisberger said. "So I've just got to go and play my game and, hopefully, win the football game."

As for any comparison to Marino, Roethlisberger said that should wait for, oh, another 15 years or so. Marino threw for 61,361 yards during his 17-season NFL career, or nearly 10,000 yards more than any other quarterback in league history.

"Obviously, it's quite a compliment coming from Coach Parcells," Roethlisberger said. "Being a guy who's been around a long time, he knows talent. But if I've said it once I've said it a million times, it's only been three games. It's a little too early to be putting those statements on it.

"If I can be half as good as Marino, I'll be incredibly happy."

Roethlisberger is only the fourth non-replacement rookie quarterback since the NFL merger in 1970 to win his first three NFL starts.

He has enjoyed a far better debut than the last Steelers first-round quarterback to start as a rookie—Bradshaw, who had only six touchdown passes and 24 interceptions in 1970.

Now Roethlisberger will try to do what no Steelers quarterback since Bradshaw has done by winning in Dallas. The Steelers are 0-2 there since the Bradshaw-led Steelers won their 1982 opener there 36-28 on a Monday night, Gary Anderson's first game as their kicker.

Roethlisberger expects to see a lot more blitzing from the Cowboys than he got from the Browns, who blitzed him only a half-dozen times and instead waited for him to make mistakes.

"You never know exactly what you're going to face, but we've seen some things where they probably will bring some all-out blitzes at us and try to use their secondary (to make plays)," Roethlisberger said. "It definitely will be a challenge."

"If I can be half as good as Marino, I'll be incredibly happy."

—Ben Roethlisberger

Aaron Josefczyk/Icon SMI

Roethlisberger Keeps Shining

Steelers 24, Cowboys 20

By Jim Vertuno *Associated Press*
October 18, 2004

The Dallas Cowboys spent a week comparing Steelers rookie quarterback Ben Roethlisberger to a young Dan Marino.

How about some Terry Bradshaw to go with it? Roethlisberger completed 21 of 25 passes and two touchdowns, completing nine straight throws on the Steelers' last two scoring drives Sunday and 11 in one stretch, leading Pittsburgh to a 24-20 comeback win over the Cowboys.

Cowboys coach Bill Parcells had warned his team about how good Roethlisberger could be. It was Parcells who compared him to Marino.

"He can flat-out play," said Steelers receiver Plaxico Burress. "I think Parcells was right."

Roethlisberger is the first rookie quarterback to go 4-0 since Phil Simms on the 1979 New York Giants. He also became the first Pittsburgh quarterback to win in Dallas since Bradshaw in 1982.

"He's got great poise," Parcells said. "I think he's going to be outstanding. I haven't changed my mind about that."

And while a rookie led the way, it was a timely Dallas fumble and a short TD from a Steelers old-timer that provided Pittsburgh (5-1) with the winning points.

The Cowboys (2-3) had the ball on the Steelers 47 and facing third down with a 20-17 lead with under 3 minutes left.

When Testaverde dropped back to pass, James Farrior, who had two sacks and caused two other fumbles, crashed through the line to knock the ball loose again. Kimo von Oelhoffen scooped it up and ran to the Dallas 24 to set up the winning drive.

The Steelers drove to the 2 and Jerome Bettis rumbled in for the final touchdown in the last minute.

"We made a mistake and it cost us big-time," Parcells said.

ABOVE: Ben Roethlisberger readies his team at the line of scrimmage. With the 24-20 come-from-behind win, he became the first Pittsburgh quarterback to win in Dallas since Terry Bradshaw did so in 1982.
James D. Smith/Icon SMI

The Cowboys (2-3) had one last chance to win with some razzle-dazzle. Dallas covered 30 yards on a pass and lateral that moved the ball to the Pittsburgh 30 with one second left. But Testaverde's final throw into the end zone fell incomplete.

"That one big mistake at the end cost us," said Testaverde, who was 23 of 36 for 284 yards. "If we hold onto the ball, the worst case we punt and they have to go 80 yards for either a touchdown or a field goal to tie."

Farrior was grateful.

"We had a little present today," Farrior said. "But we'll take it and we appreciate it."

The Steelers have won four in a row. And it will be Roethlisberger, the cool rookie who stood in the pocket and made some tough throws against a rugged pass rush, who will be credited with guiding them to this one.

"I was trying not to get hurt," said Roethlisberger, who was sacked three times but avoided several others. "I was able to make some people miss and luckily I have the best receivers in the game."

BELOW: En route to completing 21 of 25 passes, Roethlisberger displays poise in the pocket while looking for a receiver. *Karl Wright/Icon SMI*

ABOVE: Despite corner back Pete Hunter's interference, Plaxico Burress pulls in a miraculous catch. *Karl Wright/Icon SMI*

Roethlisberger was sharp at the outset. After Richie Anderson capped the Cowboys' first drive with a 21-yard TD run, the Steelers marched downfield to tie it on Roethlisberger's five-yard pass to Burress.

In that one play, Roethlisberger showed more mobility than Marino ever did, scrambling out of the pocket to his right and slinging the ball to Burress an instant before Marcellus Wiley tackled him from behind.

The play excited the many Steelers fans sprinkled throughout Texas Stadium who waved their signature "Terrible Towels" with every first down.

"For a minute there I thought we were in Pittsburgh," said Cowboys linebacker Dexter

Coakley. "It felt like it was a home game for them."

The Cowboys led 13-10 in the third period when Testaverde connected with Keyshawn Johnson on a 22-yard TD. But the Steelers made it 20-17 on Roethlisberger's TD pass to Jerame Tuman when he stood flat-footed in the pocket and rifled the ball to the back of the end zone.

"There was no panic," said Hines Ward, who led the Steelers with nine catches. "He showed a lot of poise and relied on the veteran guys around him."

BELOW: Defensive tackle Kimo von Oelhoffen (67) celebrates his fumble recovery in the last quarter. The recovery and run set up the winning drive for the Steelers. *James D. Smith/Icon SMI*

> **"There was no panic. He showed a lot of poise and relied on the veteran guys around him."**
>
> —Hines Ward

The Cowboys had their chance to close it out before the final fumble. But the Steelers weren't going to let Testaverde have a free shot at a first down.

"We had to blitz," said Steelers coach Bill Cowher. "We couldn't let Vinny just sit back there and get into a rhythm. We had to find a way to disrupt him."

ABOVE: The Steelers mob Jerome Bettis after his touchdown run from the two-yard line clinched the game, 24-20. *James D. Smith/Icon SMI*

Big Ben Defies Rookie Comparisons

Behind rookie QB who wasn't supposed to play, Steelers among NFL surprises

By Alan Robinson *Associated Press*

October 21, 2004

The day he was drafted, Ben Roethlisberger was compared to Terry Bradshaw, the last Pittsburgh Steelers quarterback chosen as early in the first round as Roethlisberger was.

The day Roethlisberger signed his first NFL contract, agent Leigh Steinberg compared him to John Elway and Troy Aikman, saying the former Miami of Ohio star owned the leadership skills, strong arm and intangibles only a few quarterbacks ever possess. Barely a week ago, Dallas Cowboys coach Bill Parcells compared him to Dan Marino, saying no rookie quarterback has so impressed him since Marino broke in with the Miami Dolphins in 1983.

Now, as the Steelers take the weekend off before meeting what arguably are the NFL's two best teams, the Patriots and Eagles, on successive weeks, they and the rest of the league seem to be running out of comparisons for Roethlisberger.

"The kid is riding an all-time high," wide receiver Hines Ward said.

Not all time, but close.

Roethlisberger is 4-0 as a starter since replacing the injured Tommy Maddox during a 30-13 loss at Baltimore on Sept. 19; the only

"The kid is riding an all-time high."

—Hines Ward

James D. Smith/Icon SMI

better start by an NFL rookie QB since the 1970 merger was by Pittsburgh's Mike Kruczek (6-0) in 1976. The difference is nobody dared to think Bradshaw could be replaced long-term by Kruczek, a caretaker quarterback who didn't throw a single touchdown pass while mostly handing off to twin 1,000-yard rushers Franco Harris and Rocky Bleier.

Today, even Bradshaw favorably compares Roethlisberger to himself, saying the rookie looks like he could be Pittsburgh's quarterback for the next 15 years. It's not just because Roethlisberger has done nothing but win, but also how he's gone about it, displaying the poise, calmness and polish rarely seen in a rookie.

"It's only been four games," Roethlisberger said. "It's a little too early to be putting statements on it like that."

But what a four-game stretch it's been, with comeback wins over the Bengals and Cowboys — the Steelers' first win in Dallas since 1982. While fellow rookie quarterbacks Eli Manning and Phillip Rivers have yet to play much, Roethlisberger is fourth in passer rating, trailing only the far more experienced Daunte Culpepper, Peyton Manning and Donovan McNabb. His 69 percent completion

ABOVE: Ben Roethlisberger put forth a valiant effort and led the Steelers to an important win over Dallas.
James D. Smith/Icon SMI

RIGHT: Roethlisberger manages to get a pass away under heavy pressure from the Dallas defense. *Karl Wright/Icon SMI*

rate would be exceptional for any quarterback, much less one who was supposed to spend all or most of this season on the bench.

Roethlisberger's effect on a team coming off a 6-10 season has been immediate and dramatic. It can easily be argued that no Steelers rookie since linebacker Jack Lambert in 1974 has made such a difference so quickly.

Certainly, the Steelers have benefited from a favorable schedule, losing to the only winning-record team they've played, Baltimore. Their schedule toughens during the final 10 weeks, with all three remaining unbeatens to play — the Patriots (5-0), Eagles (5-0) and Jets (5-0) — plus the Giants (4-1), Jaguars (4-2), Ravens (3-2) and division rivals Cleveland (3-3) and Cincinnati (1-4) on the road. They'll also be without injured nose tackle Casey Hampton (knee) for the rest of the season and cornerback Chad Scott (knee) for much of it.

Still, the confidence Roethlisberger has quickly built among his teammates is obvious. A year after they lost five times by a touchdown or less, the Steelers have rallied to win three times in the fourth quarter.

"Momentum is such a big thing," coach Bill Cowher said. "It can create confidence. We are a very confident football team. Maybe we are more confident than we are good. Right now, these guys believe in each other and they believe they will find a way to win."

The Steelers' turnaround—they will equal last season's victory total with their next win—isn't totally traceable to Roethlisberger. The running game, the NFL's second-worst last season, is again among the upper quarter of the league after adding running back Duce Staley, who already has three 100-yard games.

The defense also has been much better under defensive coordinator Dick LeBeau, who has brought back the pressure and blitzing the Steelers used so successfully in the mid-1990s. One of those blitzes led to Dallas quarterback Vinny Testaverde's fumble that was turned into the winning touchdown during the Steelers' 24-20 victory Sunday. It was Pittsburgh's 15th forced turnover, only 10 fewer than in 16 games last season.

But it's Roethlisberger who has created the biggest stir in a city that never needs much of an excuse to get excited about the Steelers. Want to guess how many Roethlisberger No. 7 jerseys will be unwrapped under western Pennsylvania Christmas trees in two months?

"I can't say enough about him," Cowher said.

> ## "Momentum is such a big thing. It can create confidence. We are a very confident team. Maybe we are more confident than we are good. Right now, these guys believe in each other and they believe they will find a way to win."
>
> —Bill Cowher

RIGHT: Thanks to his exceptional skill as a quarterback, Ben Roethlisberger has received accolades from coaches and players across the league.
Karl Wright/Icon SMI

Roethlisberger Making It Look Easy

Steelers 34, Patriots 20

By Alan Robinson *Associated Press*

November 1, 2004

This was the game that would expose Ben Roethlisberger as just another rookie. Surely, he couldn't handle the Patriots' complex and innovative defense, or the pressure of trying to end the NFL's longest winning streak ever.

Maybe somebody should tell the Pittsburgh rookie quarterback it's not supposed to be this easy, not even for a player whose own winning streak is nearly as long as the New England streak he just ended. Proving he can be just as good against a Bill Belichick-coached team as he is against the Browns and the Bengals, Roethlisberger played like an imperturbable veteran—something two-time Super Bowl winner Tom Brady of New England did not do—in Pittsburgh's surprisingly easy 34-20 victory Sunday.

Just like that, the Patriots' 21-game winning streak and NFL-record 18-game regular-season run ended, largely because of a rookie who further enhanced his ever-growing repu-

tation by making the defending Super Bowl champions look very ordinary.

Roethlisberger became the first quarterback to win his first five NFL starts since the Steelers' Mike Kruczek was 6-0 in 1976, completing 18 of 24 passes for 196 yards and two touchdowns. In his last two games, he's 39 of 49—the kind of numbers associated with a quarterback in a low-risk West Coast offense, not one that constantly looks to get the ball downfield to ace receivers Hines Ward and Plaxico Burress.

"I heard those experts talking on TV that he can't beat a Bill Belichick defense," said Plaxico Burress, who connected with Roethlisberger on two first-quarter touchdown pass plays as Pittsburgh opened a 21-3 lead. "But they're finding out around the league."

Here's what they're learning: the Patriots (6-1) might not necessarily be the team to beat in the AFC, not with the Steelers (6-1) off to

ABOVE: Ben Roethlisberger tries to shed Patriots linebacker Mike Vrabel. *Jason Cohn/Icon SMI*

their best start since their 1978 Super Bowl champions started 7-0.

"It definitely was a statement game for us," Steelers linebacker Joey Porter said. "Each game gets bigger."

He's not kidding. After becoming the first team to beat the Patriots since Washington edged them 20-17 on Sept. 28, 2003, the Steelers will face the NFL's only remaining unbeaten team, Philadelphia (7-0), on Sunday.

Surely, Roethlisberger couldn't take out what arguably are the NFL's two best teams in as many weeks—or could he?

"You can't describe his effort," receiver Hines Ward said. "He's 5-0, and he's earning a lot of respect on this team. The guys on this team are fighting hard for him."

No doubt the Steelers got a big lift when they learned that Corey Dillon, coming off consecutive 100-yard games, was being held out with a thigh injury. They got another one when Pro Bowl cornerback Ty Law injured his left foot in the first quarter, allowing Roethlisberger and Burress to pick on backup Randall Gay for a 47-yard scoring pass play.

Brady's turnovers on consecutive New England plays—a fumble and Deshea Townsend's 39-yard interception return for a touchdown—quickly made it 21-3 later in the first quarter. By then, New England fans were realizing that, on the same week the Red Sox

BELOW: Plaxico Burress reels in another amazing catch. Rowthlisberger and Burress connected for two first-quarter touchdowns against the Pats. *Jason Cohn/Icon SMI*

won the World Series, maybe it was too much to expect all this winning to continue.

"It was never about the streak, that was never part of our preparation," linebacker Mike Vrabel said. "It wasn't this week against the Steelers, either—we just didn't play well enough to win, that's it."

With Dillon out and the Patriots way behind early, they didn't even try to run back-up Kevin Faulk; their six rushing attempts were three fewer than the franchise's previous

BELOW: A fired-up Ben Roethlisberger congratulates his offensive line as they come off the field. *Jason Cohn/Icon SMI*

> ## "You can't describe his effort. He's 5-0, and he's earning a lot of respect on this team. The guys on this team are fighting hard for him."
>
> —Hines Ward

single-game low in a 1996 game against Denver.

"We got behind to a very good team," Brady said. "We made it tough on ourselves. We dug ourselves a big ditch and we couldn't find our way out of it."

BELOW: During a break in the action, Roethlisberger checks the scoreboard and finds the Steelers on top.
Jason Cohn/Icon SMI

Jason Cohn/Icon SMI

Roethlisberger Record Rolls Along

Rookie QB has Steelers off to best start since the 1970s

By Alan Robinson *Associated Press*

November 1, 2004

He wasn't yet born the last time the Pittsburgh Steelers won the Super Bowl. That isn't preventing rookie quarterback Ben Roethlisberger from bringing back the memories of the greatest times—and the greatest teams—in franchise history.

The Steelers are 6-1 after ending New England's 21-game winning streak with a dominating 34-20 victory Sunday in which Roethlisberger improved to 5-0 as a starter. In a fitting throwback to the days when the Steelers won four Super Bowls in six seasons, Roethlisberger is off to the best start by an NFL rookie quarterback since Pittsburgh's Mike Kruczek was 6-0 in 1976. "We have a rookie quarterback who is playing tremendous," linebacker Joey Porter said.

The Steelers need him to keep playing that well Sunday against the Philadelphia Eagles (7-0) as they try to accomplish something no NFL team has done so late in a season: beat undefeated teams in successive weeks.

Just playing unbeaten teams in consecutive games past the early weeks of a season is a rare-enough occurrence; it hasn't happened since the Detroit Lions lost twice to the undefeated Chicago Bears to close out the 1934 season. It also occurred in 1921, when Dayton played Akron (7-0-1) and Buffalo (7-0-2), and in 1920, when Canton met Buffalo (7-0) and Akron (6-0-1).

"Everybody's antennas across the country are starting to go up a little bit," wide receiver Plaxico Burress said, referring to the Steelers' new-found notoriety.

That's largely because of a 22-year-old quarterback who plays like he's much, much older. Because of Roethlisberger, the Steelers, an out-of-the-running 6-10 only a season ago, are hearing about all this ancient history:

—They are off to their best seven-game start in Bill Cowher's 13 seasons as coach; they've been 5-2 five times. It's also their best start since a franchise-best 7-0 in 1978, the season they won the third of their four Super Bowls.

—The Steelers have made the playoffs every other season they were 6-1 or better (1978, 1975, 1974, 1973) and won the Super Bowl three of those four seasons.

—Concidentally or not, the Steelers will recognize the 25th anniversary of their last Super Bowl championship team by saluting the 1979 Steelers on Sunday. Hall of Famer Terry Bradshaw was the quarterback of that team, yet his 1970 rookie numbers (six touch-downs, 24 interceptions) can't compare to Roethlisberger's (70.1 completion percentage, a 104.7 passer rating, nine touchdowns, four interceptions, one interception in his last 116 passes).

"We keep saying it over and over again: Let's not get too excited," Roethlisberger said. "We're just trying to keep our focus, keep our mind on the straight and narrow, and focus on Philadelphia."

With former Eagles running back Duce Staley coming off his fourth 100-yard game, it all adds up to arguably the biggest Eagles-Steelers game since 1947. Back then, the Eagles won 21-0 in Pittsburgh in a special Eastern

Jason Cohn/Icon SMI

Jason Cohn/Icon SMI

Conference playoff game staged after the teams tied for the regular season title.

The only comparable regular-season game since the teams moved into separate conferences in 1970 came in 1979, when the Eagles surprised the Steelers 17-14. The Steelers, who would go on to win the Super Bowl, were 4-0 at the time and the Eagles, who would lose in the Super Bowl a year later, were 3-1.

Wide receiver Hines Ward doesn't think the Steelers will have any problem matching the intensity they showed against the Patriots when they meet the Eagles.

"We've got a great running game, two dominant wide receivers and a young, confident, cocky quarterback back there playing his heart out," Ward said. "We're a hard team to beat."

Cowher also doesn't think the Steelers will become distracted as they try to return to the playoffs after missing them last season and four of their previous six seasons.

"We'll be fine," he said. "We aren't going to squander what we have created for ourselves. We'll be ready to go, trust me."

One of the Best Rookies Ever?

Not beyond comparison: Marino says Big Ben reminds him of own rookie year

By Alan Robinson *Associated Press*

November 2, 2004

Dan Marino didn't say out loud what he was thinking in 1983, but it took him only a few games to become convinced he would be an excellent NFL quarterback. He is certain Pittsburgh Steelers rookie Ben Roethlisberger already feels the same way.

After hearing for weeks how his exceptional debut has reminded many of Marino's rookie season with Miami, Roethlisberger heard it from Marino himself Tuesday as the two met for a televised interview. Marino's assessment of what already is the most talked-about Steelers rookie quarterback since Terry Bradshaw in 1970: real good now, and will get even better the longer he plays.

"A lot of the things he does kind of remind me of some of the things I was able to do when I played," Marino said. "The thing that's impressive about Ben is his awareness in the pocket, his pocket presence and his ability to move and still make throws downfield. You can't teach those kind of instincts, and that's something he has going for him that a lot of the guys in the league don't have."

> "You can't teach those kind of instincts, and that's something he has going for him that a lot of the guys in the league don't have."
>
> —Dan Marino

Just as Marino looked and felt comfortable almost as soon as he took over for the benched David Woodley in 1983, Roethlisberger has appeared confident and well-prepared since replacing the injured Tommy Maddox on Sept. 19. He is 5-0 as a starter for the Steelers (6-1), the best start by an NFL rookie quarterback since Pittsburgh's Mike Kruczek was 6-0 in 1976.

"I think you realize it pretty quick," Marino said when asked how long it takes for a player to know he can play. "You get a feel for it pretty quick because you compare yourself to other people and what they've done. You might not publicly come out and say you think you're going to be a guy who can be here for a while, but I think you know as far as how you feel personally."

Does Roethlisberger feel that way after leading the Steelers past New England 34-20 Sunday, ending the Patriots' 21-game winning streak?

"There's no doubt," said Marino, the NFL career passing leader with 61,361 yards. "Because of what he's done, he's right there. The performance is there, the winning, and they've got one of the better teams in the league. They just beat the team that was 21-0, so all that contributes to a high

Mike Simons/Icon SMI

Aaron Josefczyk/Icon SMI

level of confidence—not only with him, but also the team around him."

Roethlisberger learned Tuesday from coach Bill Cowher what already was a foregone conclusion: Even after Maddox is healthy again, perhaps as early as this week, Roethlisberger is the starter.

Roethlisberger isn't throwing as much as Marino did in 1983, when he was 173-of-296 for 2,210 yards, 20 touchdowns and six interceptions in 11 games. The Dolphins went 12-4 and made the playoffs, then reached the Super Bowl a year later after going 14-2.

Roethlisberger is 96 of 137 for 1,133 yards, nine touchdowns and four interceptions in six games, but has only two interceptions in his five starts. His 70.1 completion percentage is on pace to easily surpass Marino's rookie record of 58.45 percent.

"He's not turning the ball over ... and that's more important than completion percentage," Marino said. "That's the biggest thing a quarterback has to deal with and worry about. He pretty much played a perfect game the other day where he made the throws he had to make, they were running the clock and getting first downs and controlling the clock, and that's a great thing to watch."

Marino thinks Roethlisberger is good enough to take his team to the Super Bowl, something no rookie quarterback has done.

"With the type of team they have, sure," Marino said. "They have guys on the outside (wide receivers Hines Ward and Plaxico Burress), they have guys who can run the football—Duce (Staley) is a solid back—(they have) the offensive line and they can get to the quarterback on defense. They definitely can get there."

ABOVE: Coach Bill Cowher offers some encouragement and instruction to rookie QB Ben Roethlisberger.
Mike Simons/Icon SMI

Well-timed Win for Steelers

Tick, Tock ... Big Ben Beats the Clock

By Mark Long *Associated Press*

December 7, 2004

Ben Roethlisberger has practiced the same scenario nearly every day since training camp.

He has 1:47 remaining, no timeouts and needs a field goal to win.

No wonder he made it look so easy Sunday night.

The rookie quarterback engineered a drive that set up Jeff Reed's 37-yard field goal with 18 seconds to play that gave the Pittsburgh Steelers a 17-16 victory over Jacksonville and extended their winning streak to 10 games.

"It's something special what he's doing," guard Alan Faneca said. "Is a rookie quarterback supposed to win a game like that on the road in a hostile environment in prime time? Probably not. That says a lot about him. He's special."

The drive covered 56 yards in six plays after Josh Scobee made a 36-yard field goal with 1:55 left to put the Jags ahead.

Roethlisberger was three of four for 39 yards on the winning drive, and his only incompletion came on a spike after he calmly

> **"Is a rookie quarterback supposed to win a game like that on the road in a hostile environment in prime time? Probably not. That says a lot about. He's special."**
>
> —Alan Faneca

ABOVE: Kicker Jeff Reed (3) and defensive back Russell Stuvaints celebrate Reed's game-winning fielc

ABOVE: After nailing the winning field goal, Jeff Reed receives a hug from Ben Roethlisberger.
Grant Halverson/Getty Images

let the clock run down to leave the Jaguars with little time for a comeback.

"I want the ball in my hands," said Roethlisberger, who set a record for most wins by a rookie quarterback. "I want to have control of the outcome of the game."

He had plenty of help, too.

Lee Mays made two huge catches, Reed drilled the kick and coach Bill Cowher effectively managed the clock.

Cowher used all three timeouts before the two-minute warning as Jacksonville was driving for the go-ahead field goal, preserving plenty of time for his offense.

Nonetheless, Roethlisberger got much of the credit.

"He did a phenomenal job standing in the pocket and staying composed," said receiver Hines Ward. "That's one of his characteristics."

Roethlisberger was 14 of 17 for 221 yards and two touchdowns. He also ran for 40 yards after three rather sluggish games in an otherwise brilliant first season.

Jacksonville (6-6) had one last shot after a 19-yard completion from Byron Leftwich to Jimmy Smith, which gave Scobee a shot at a 60-yarder. It fell just short and wide right.

"I thought I had it, but it doesn't matter if you miss it by 100 feet or one foot," Scobee said.

The Steelers (10-1) are one win from clinching the AFC North and hold a tiebreaker for home-field advantage in the AFC over the New England Patriots. They also hold a four-game lead over Baltimore with four games left.

Jacksonville, which could have moved into a tie with Baltimore and Denver for the final AFC wild-card spot, lost its third in a row and remains a game behind those two.

> "He did a phenomenal job standing in the pocket and staying composed. That's one of his characteristics."
>
> —Hines Ward

Jason Cohn/Icon SMI

Perfect 10

Roethlisberger leads game-winning drive as Steelers beat Jags 17-16

By *The Associated Press*

December 6, 2004

Ben Roethlisberger had plenty of help in pulling off the first last-minute drive of his career.

The rookie quarterback extended both his and Pittsburgh's winning streak to 10 games by engineering a late drive Sunday night to set up a 37-yard field goal by Jeff Reed with 18 seconds left that gave the Steelers a 17-16 win over Jacksonville on Sunday night.

The drive, the kind pulled off multiple times by stars like John Elway, Dan Marino and Joe Montana, covered 56 yards in six plays after Josh Scobee made a 36-yard field goal with 1:55 left that gave the Jaguars the lead.

Roethlisberger said that the Steelers' regular two-minute drill routine is to put 1:47 on the clock and play with no timeouts and needing a field goal.

"I want the ball in my hands," he said. "I want to have control of the outcome of the game."

But the young quarterback, who set a record for most wins by a rookie quarterback, wasn't the only star of the last-minute victory.

Reed drilled the kick, of course. And the win by the Steelers (10-1) was a testament to coach Bill Cowher's clock management. He used all three of his timeouts before the two-minute warning as Jacksonville was driving for the go-ahead field goal, preserving plenty of time for his offense.

Then Roethlisberger was three of four for 39 yards on the winning drive, and the one incompletion was a spike after he calmly let the clock run down to avoid giving the Jaguars much time for a march of their own.

.... xiously as officials review

ABOVE: Wide receiver Hines Ward celebrates after scoring on a 37-yard reception. Quarterback Ben Roethlisberger completed 14 of 17 passes against the Jaguars. *Grant Halverson/Getty Images*

He finished the night 14 of 17 for 221 yards and two touchdowns and had a passer rating of 158, just three-tenths of a point from perfection. He also rushed for 40 yards after three rather sluggish games in an otherwise brilliant rookie year.

Jacksonville (6-6) had one last shot after a 19-yard completion from Byron Leftwich to Jimmy Smith, which gave Scobee a shot at a 60-yarder. It fell just short and wide right.

"We had opportunities," Jaguars coach Jack Del Rio said. "One play—and we had any number of chances at a play—and we'd be a whole lot happier right now. It didn't happen."

ABOVE: It takes a pack of Jaguars to bring down running back Jerome Bettis. *Grant Halverson/Getty Images*

The Steelers are one win from clinching the AFC North and hold a tiebreaker for home-field advantage in the AFC over the New England Patriots, whom they handed their only loss. They hold a four-game lead over Baltimore with four games left, but their only loss of the season was to the Ravens, when veteran quarterback Tommy Maddox was injured and Roethlisberger took over.

Jacksonville, which could have moved into a tie with Baltimore and Denver for the final AFC wild-card spot, remains a game behind those two. The Jaguars have had 11 of their 12 games decided in the final minute.

Pittsburgh scored touchdowns on its first two possessions, but was held without a point for the rest of the game until the final drive.

In the first three quarters, the Jags moved inside the Pittsburgh 15 three times, but came out with only six points—Scobee missed a 32-yard field-goal attempt in the second quarter and made two others.

"It was as tough a loss as we've had since the AFC championship game in 1999," said wide receiver Jimmy Smith, who has been with the Jaguars since their founding as an expansion team 10 seasons ago.

LEFT: After kicking the winning field goal, Jeff Reed rushes to the sideline to celebrate with his teammates. *Grant Halverson/Getty Images*

The first Steelers TD came after a 77-yard, seven-play drive when Roethlisberger hit Hines Ward for a 37-yard score.

Leftwich, who finished 16 of 27 for 268 yards, countered with a 12-play, 73-yard drive, finding Troy Edwards from 22 yards. As Ward did on the first TD, Edwards broke a tackle and ran in for the score.

Pittsburgh made it 14-7 on Roethlisberger's 26-yard pass to tight end Jay Riemersma to cap a 72-yard drive.

Jacksonville cut it to 14-10 on Scobee's 20-yard field goal on its first second-half possession, in which it went from its 2 to the Pittsburgh 2. There were two big plays on the drive: a 56-yard pass from Leftwich to third-string tight end Todd Yoder and a 36-yarder to Edwards.

Scobee's 29-yarder in the final seconds of the third quarter made it 14-13.

RIGHT: Ben Roethlisberger and the Steelers wait on the sideline to celebrate their win with kicker Jeff Reed. *Grant Halverson/Getty Images*

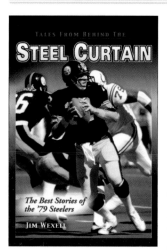

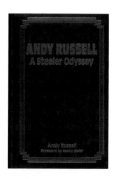

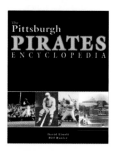
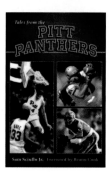
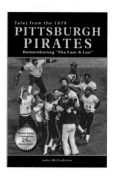